ALIGN YOUR BRAND WITH SOCIAL IMPACT

The 5-Step Process to Massive Growth and Sustainability

Tabia Pope, Ph.D., CCC-SLP

The Host of BIA BRAND® with Dr. Tabia Pope

Table of Contents

DEDICATION

We are either getting ready to go into the process, we're in the process, or we're coming out of the process. This book is dedicated to social entrepreneurs transforming lives through image, communications, health, wellness, or lifestyle. You are getting ready to go into the process, or you are in the process of restructuring, rebranding, and realigning your business or even businesses with social impact. I was there at one point, so I understand your needs! This book is for all those who are committing to the process. I hope this book gives you the confidence you need to build a social impact brand for a nonprofit organization or socially responsible business. Let this book help you understand where to start within my 5-Step Process. Give yourself time and grace as you work towards achieving massive growth and sustainability. This book is only the beginning of my conversation with you throughout your journey to aligning your brand with social impact.

This book pays homage to my own journey and the journey of all of the social entrepreneurs who were inspired to activate their role in the process of social impact branding. Whether they started working inside an organization or company, as a consultant, or as an entrepreneur, they believed enough in their purpose, cause, vision, and mission and how it would impact the community they serve. I would not have known it was possible if not for all of the social entrepreneurs who have come before me and branded themselves in this way. They have shown me how to use their influence to persuade an audience to purchase services and products, increase their knowledge, and change their attitudes towards raising awareness and donations for issues related to image, communications, health, wellness, or lifestyle. When you align your brand with social impact, you'll be even more successful at advocacy, outreach, education, collaboration, counseling, prevention, and wellness! When we support each other's causes, we can achieve more! So, I am here to support your purpose, cause, vision, and mission and see that your brand gets through this process perfectly aligned with social impact!

THE JOURNEY

"She had to make sure everybody understood her God-given assignment – her purpose for taking up this space, her passion for her work, and her causes that mattered to her. She had to make sure that she delivered clear brand messaging and conducted the market research to understand her audiences."

Dr. Pope was making a 6 figure salary as a Speech-Language Pathologist and Director of Rehabilitation, but she found herself at one of the lowest moments of her budding career because her brand was misaligned. She found herself being overworked for a company whose mission didn't align with her core brand values, purpose, causes, vision, and mission. She worked 10-hours in a day and sometimes weekends during the pandemic, balancing being a wife and mother of two toddlers and juggling to launch her non-profit organization, Head to Speech, and restructure, re-brand, and realign BIA Communications to support her transition into social entrepreneurship.

TAKE THE LEAP: She found herself physically present but suffering from back pain and becoming increasingly mentally checked out. She daydreamed about her two businesses becoming aligned and being nationally recognized for social impact branding through educational, scientific, and charitable initiatives. Due to this, the lack of time and flexibility weighed the title and salary at this point. Although she wasn't ready financially to take the leap, she was physically and emotionally ready to invest the time needed to complete it. In fact, when she realized that her life was so out of alignment, it made it even easier to say no to unrealistic expectations. She quit her full-time job with the support of her family and start-up donors and vowed to commit to aligning her brand with the causes that mattered the most to her and her community!

UNDERSTAND THE ASSIGNMENT: Even with her community's support, it was not easy. She still had to work as-needed jobs as a speech-language pathologist in healthcare settings. She had to evaluate every opportunity presented to her as Head to Speech evolved, and BIA Communications helped to support her through in-kind resources and donations through consulting and speaking engagements. She did not want to provide only services and products; she wanted to make an impact within the communities that she cared most about. She had to ensure everybody understood her God-given assignment – her purpose for taking up this space, her passion for her work, and the causes that mattered to her. She had to ensure that she delivered clear brand messaging and conducted the market research to understand her audiences. By aligning herself with brands who appreciated her passion for preventative education, advocacy, policy and community outreach, and health literacy, she knew she would accelerate everything she wanted to accomplish. She also started evaluating opportunities regarding how well they aligned with her scholarship, teaching, and service. She knew that the institutions, partners, sponsors, and donors that aligned in this way would allow her to achieve massive growth and sustainability both personally and professionally.

WALKING IN YOUR PURPOSE: All of the chaos she had gone through previously because her brand was misaligned wasn't in vain. She trusted in God's plan during her period of misalignment. She really had to honor her intuition and believe that was God's way of telling her to continue to work on her businesses even with limited resources. She continued to be obedient, work hard, and walk in with her purpose no matter what. One day a sense of peace came over her when the opportunity finally came for her to align her purpose, cause, vision, and mission to her scholarship, teaching, and service within a university setting. God opened the door for her as a Professor to build a specialty clinic and to have Head to Speech become a community partner. BIA Communications continued to grow through coaching, consulting, publishing books, and speaking engagements. A percentage of proceeds from these opportunities helped to sustain Head to Speech. She walked into the next chapter of her life with more purpose and passion for her cause, vision, and mission. She wouldn't have been able to achieve this level of alignment without pursuing her niche and being specific about how she would influence her key audience and lead her Ambassadors within the global community. She was able to build a foundation for her brand and maintain the brand by aligning the brand with social impact. Now, the rest is history!

CHAPTER 1

IS YOUR BRAND ALIGNED WITH SOCIAL IMPACT?

Most of us get so caught up in the bright lights of having a business that we completely overlook the most important process of our brand identity: authenticity. By reading this book, you will find that I will teach you the art of authentic personal branding as it relates to your purpose, cause, vision, and mission. Coined by Dr. Hubert Rampersad, authentic personal branding is holistic and measurable. You need to demonstrate a level of self-awareness of your own internal and external transformation. I ask you to take time to understand and identify with the real you and how it relates to aligning your brand with social impact as a social entrepreneur and influencer. Dive deep into your values, strengths, personality traits, and story. Then put your true self out there and consciously shape how you are recognized and remembered. I love that personal branding is an ongoing process of developing and maintaining an impression or track record. I also love the self-packaging aspect of branding. You will know if your personal brand is successful at alignment by being able to self-package your unique combination of skills, experience, and personality surrounding social responsibility.

By reading this book, you will explore how social responsibility is a type of business self-regulation that aims at keeping your brand socially accountable towards itself, board members, advisors, partners, sponsors, donors, ambassadors, volunteers, the community, and the environment. According to Investopedia, sustainability is the ability to maintain or support a process continuously over time. Implementing environmental, philanthropic, diversity, equity and inclusion, and economic programs allows your brand to drive positive change and contribute to tackling issues related to being eco-friendly, creating traditions of giving of one's time, talent, and treasure, strengthening diversity, equity, and inclusion within communities, and empowering the next generation through economic and business solutions. The idea is for your brand to give back to society by volunteering, enhancing operations, funding projects, or fighting for causes that look after people within your community and the global community.

If you are anything like me, you transform lives through image, communications, health, wellness, and lifestyle industries. Social responsibility and public health issues related to your work should be at the forefront because you impact your clients, patients, customers, students, and the community. They come to you for advice, support, and counseling. You are driven by the opportunity to enhance their extrinsic qualities. Their support of your work is also driven by the social causes you support and incorporate into your work-life balance.

We all have a brand and social responsibility whether we like it or not. You may recognize your brand and execute your social responsibility while others do not. You may recognize that aligning your brand with social impact allows your audience to see a different side of you and your business. Your brand will be seen as more than just a name, logo, or tagline. It will be seen as a force of change that will enhance your online presence and reputation. It's about telling your brand's story so it stands out by implementing social responsibility as part of your brand activities and the stories of those with whom your brand impacts. If there's a cause or social mission you care about, why not make it something that helps you build your business and spread your message?

I believe everyone has a story. Sharing your story permits others to do the same. Tapping into what your clients, patients, customers, or consumers are dealing with will allow you to discover the problem, find a solution, and help them take the action they need now to advocate for their own transformation. Subsequently, by helping others, we help ourselves. We can get so busy with transforming everyone else's brand and often neglect our own brand and the opportunities to promote causes that matter to us. Aligning your brand with social impact will help you make new connections, discover new opportunities, and reveal your true self within a community that understands your story.

Whether you're an established social entrepreneur or emerging into your new role, social impact branding will not only contribute to social good but also helps you increase your brand awareness and content marketing and your brand value. By reading this book, you will come to understand how digital marketing on social media is worthless for your brand building if there's no emotional connection with your audience. In fact, your community cares more about how your brand makes them feel than the actual product or service itself. An effective social impact strategy, including a healthy communications plan, can help you build a strong brand using video marketing. This strategy is essential for nonprofits and for-profit social ventures of all sizes and missions and lies at the core of many public health policies.

We may be good at promoting our services and products, but we often forget that we have a larger role to play within our communities. Social impact branding is an approach that connects your actions and influence beyond products or services to address a local or global community need through systemic, sustainable, and innovative policies, initiatives, or programs. By aligning your brand with social impact, you can affect people within the surrounding community directly or people in different communities, states, and even countries. When you lead with social impact, you are making a conscious effort to not only invest in making a positive change but also to build deeper bonds with existing consumers, expand the consumer base and enlist those brand ambassadors to share your brand message. When people see your brand's positive impact and realize you're still a successful brand, they will understand that you are not afraid to show the world what you stand for and use your platform to encourage others to do the same. Don't talk about changing the world; you do it and get others to follow your lead.

Social impact branding is often the missing link between the customer experience and the bottom line. Choosing to be driven by a cause, purpose, vision, and mission elevates your brand, sustains your business, and helps to achieve massive growth. The 21st century measures economic value not only by sales and profits but also by social responsibility. Your target audience wants to feel good about supporting, purchasing, and sharing your courses, programs, products, and services because it uses a portion of the profits, operations, or purpose to improve the quality of life for others. Focusing on the common good doesn't prevent you from making a profit, but it requires making every decision with both criteria in mind.

Brand alignment means that all elements of your social impact strategy – the needs of your community, the structure of your business, sustainable goals, social responsibility, and social marketing plan are arranged in such a way as to best support the fulfillment of your purpose, cause, vision, and mission. Alignment is a continuous linear process as there are ongoing changes to your community's needs, organizational structures, initiatives, and strategies, but your cause, purpose, vision, and mission remain the same. The fastest way to align your brand with social impact is to visually connect elements of your brand with other elements within your community.

Your cause, purpose, vision, and mission are unclear when your brand is out of alignment. You will accept opportunities that work against your brand's massive growth and sustainability. Consequently, leading to decreased time to develop and nurture the right network to build capacity and resources that help to further your vision, carry out your brand strategies, and accomplish your mission's goals and objectives. Your brand will also be unable to collect the necessary data you need to demonstrate the positive outcomes of your brand's social impact. If your brand isn't able to demonstrate its assets or package and sell its story to others, it will be difficult to expand its reach, influence, revenue, and visibility.

I have used these foundational concepts within my own life and with my client experiences to guide them through my 5-Step Process of aligning your brand with social impact. By reading this book, you will begin to take the necessary steps to achieve massive growth and sustainability. I want you to take a moment to consider how each step can help you develop, implement, and evaluate the areas of your brand that need to be aligned with social impact. I want you to manifest those opportunities that are aligned with social impact so that you can achieve massive growth and sustainability at an accelerated pace.

The business case for social impact has never been stronger because it makes a difference in attracting talent and retaining satisfied individuals, businesses, and organizations to want to work with your brand. The competitive advantage ultimately differentiates your brand from other competitors, increases brand awareness, improves your bottom line, and provides far greater opportunities to benefit the community. By the end of reading this book, you will have clarity and know what you want to achieve. I look forward to finding what you want to achieve and how I can help you stay committed to the process once we connect.

Massive growth and sustainability for your brand may look like this…

- Connecting on a deeper level with your clients, patients, employees, customers, or community as a business owner, social entrepreneur, or influencer

- Reaching more people within your community to help them environmentally, socially, culturally, or economically

- Attracting employees or volunteers who are inspired, motivated, and loyal to your cause

- Growing and scaling a business built as a social enterprise, nonprofit organization or both

- Giving back your time through mentoring

- Generating more revenue through teaching

- Maximizing the visibility of your community service

- Closing more sales with customers that support your cause

- Gaining more partnerships and sponsorships

- Training more Brand Ambassadors

- Growing your brand influence

- Marketing how you align your brand with social impact

- Increased foot traffic if they're committed to supporting the local community

- Increased profitability and long-term financial success

- Growth in revenue generation in business

- Growth in sustainability, longevity, and commitment to your causes

RESOURCES AND COURSES

I have provided the following free download, resources, and courses that will help guide you as you read through the book and prepare you for your next steps throughout the process. My image and brand management talk show, BIA BRAND also covers many of the topics covered within this book. You can access, print, or read them at **biabrand.tv**. Don't forget to subscribe and watch on YouTube.

- Before diving in, I recommend you download the free *Align Your Brand with Social Impact Workbook* to keep track of your notes and ideas as you read this book. Sometimes, seeing the main points and thought questions for each chapter on just a few pages helps you understand the 5-Step Process and the bigger picture of the journey ahead of you. Join the LIVE Q & A by tuning into *"It's a Great Day Ta-BIA BRAND"* morning fireside chats by following @biabrandTV and keeping up on LinkedIn.

- Know your starting point as you read through the book by downloading the *Align Your Brand with Social Impact Assessment.* If you think you'll benefit from an in-depth assessment to help align your brand with social impact and accelerate your massive growth and sustainability. If you ask yourself the following questions, this assessment will help you examine your current brand with social impact: Where am I currently with my brand? What are my brand's unique strengths, motivators, attributes, goals, and objectives? "Is this…(e.g., service, program, product, partnership, sponsorship, or grant) aligned with my brand?

- You will be challenged to complete self-study modules at your own pace and journal prompts designed for you to get through the 5-Step Process with clarity and ease. Visualize the alignment of your brand with social impact by joining the *Align Your Brand with Social Impact Challenge*. If you are asking yourself the following questions, then these challenges, including modules, journals, and affirmation cards, will help you through your visualization and manifestation exercises: How am I going to develop my social impact? How do I define social impact? How will I pitch my vision, mission, and unique brand assets?

- Fast-track the creation of your social impact strategy action plan, including social marketing and health communications concepts with strategy sessions and writing prompts inside the **Align Your Brand with Social Impact Accelerator**. If you are asking yourself the following questions, then this accelerator group will help you transform your million-dollar ideas into brand assets that are aligned with social impact: How will my brand produce our social impact strategy? How will my brand measure and evaluate our social impact potential in order to uphold our brand promise by making an impact?

- Practice writing and speaking about how your brand is aligned with social impact and influential in raising awareness and donations for your causes and community. Focus on launching or leveraging your brand with social impact to generate results by carrying out your social impact strategy. As you join the ***BIA BRAND with Dr. Tabia Pope TV Network,*** we will increase your brand's visibility through an image management talk show experience including intensive production days and group workshops. We will practice and refine your brand story and enhance your on-camera presence, communication skills, and visual appearance for media exposure. If you are asking yourself the following questions, then becoming a guest on the show and on-camera training would help your brand raise awareness and donations for your cause and social impact initiatives: Which areas of my brand story, communication skills, visual appearance or video marketing do I need help with?

CHAPTER 2

WHY I AM SO COMMITTED
TO HELPING YOU

Some of the best advice I have to offer you is through my process of aligning both of my businesses into a brand with social impact. Even though my brand is aligned with social impact, there was a period when my brand was misaligned with my cause, purpose, vision, or mission. It is aligned now! So how did I get to this point, ultimately leading to my brand achieving massive growth and sustainability?

Let me start by telling you what most people know about me. Over the past decade, I have gone from being a healthcare Speech-Language Pathologist and struggling doctoral student to a Professor, social entrepreneur, and influencer. During this time, I founded both BIA Communications as a Limited Liability Company (LLC) and Head to Speech, Incorporated as a 501(c)(3) nonprofit organization. I expanded my brand by becoming an Ambassador for brain health, wellness, and brain injury, in addition to creating my own image management talk show to provide communication skills and image enhancement coaching. I now have two businesses representing my brand within the community, but it wasn't always that way.

When people usually hear the term Speech-Language Pathologist (SLP), they think of nonprofit organizations, such as Autism Speaks or Alzheimer's Association. However, Head to Speech® has entered this socially responsible space within the profession by advocating for the inclusion of SLPs within sports concussion management protocols to treat the effects on cognitive-communication skills, and overall brain health. We have expanded the role by addressing the social impact issues that affect athletes and their support systems. The organization goes beyond prehabilitation, brain injury, and rehabilitation because it also includes interprofessional education and collaborative practices, brain health challenges, brain workouts, concussion recovery care packages, self-care initiatives, cultural responsiveness for assessments and interventions, and healthcare disparities.

Another way I align my passion for brand, image, and authenticity into Head to Speech is by supporting athletes and their Name, Image, Likeness (NIL) initiative by training athletes to become Head to Speech Ambassadors and providing a platform for them to raise awareness about their own brain health routines or sports concussion history. We teach them to advocate for themselves and integrate brain health and dual-tasking using cognitive and physical exercises into their daily lives and workout routines. My nonprofit organization utilizes social impact branding and video marketing strategies to raise awareness and donations and conduct market research to support athletes' brain health and their support systems throughout the continuum of care and lifetime.

On the other hand, I founded BIA Communications, affectionately known as BIA Brand®, as a digital media production and social impact branding consultancy that utilizes health communications and video marketing strategies. My company has become a social enterprise as it produces the image management talk show BIA Brand with Dr. Tabia Pope. The company also financially supports Head to Speech through in-kind donations for coaching, consulting, and speaking services. BIA Communications provides on-camera communication skills and image enhancement coaching for leadership, Ambassadors, and volunteers, as well as supports my talk show guests and clients by raising awareness and donations for their causes and ours.

My colleagues now consider me a social entrepreneur and trailblazer, in addition to recognizing how I have used health communications, authentic personal branding, and social marketing strategies to increase my visibility as a national brand with social impact. Becoming known this way helped me succeed as a coach, consultant, public speaker, professor, and continuing education provider. I aligned my brand values, cause, purpose, mission, and vision to my scholarship, teaching, and service. It increased the number of opportunities I had to engage with my students and community. Since going through and developing my 5-Step Process, I have experienced massive growth by creating multiple revenue streams through courses, programs, products, speaking engagements, and media appearances.

WHAT STILL BLOWS ME AWAY ABOUT MY MASSIVE GROWTH

But let me tell you why I am still blown away by how quickly I was able to achieve massive growth as a brand with social impact. I was able to transform my award-winning and nationally recognized 300-page dissertation into the very first 501(c)(3) nonprofit organization dedicated to educational, scientific, and charitable initiatives for sports concussions, their effects on cognitive-communication skills, and overall brain health.

Within the first year, Head to Speech became an exhibitor at my professional association's national convention, which brings together approximately 15,000 attendees who are speech-language pathologists and audiologists. We launched our first interactive booth with a public service announcement challenge. Our online visibility and marketing list grew from zero to over 3,000 within months of the convention. My own social media following grew on LinkedIn to over 4,500 followers and 8,000 across platforms. My posts about my organization impacting the lives of student-athletes and their return to learning reached over 10,000 impressions.

Within the second year, I went on a speaking tour, producing continuing education courses and hosting a sports concussion Podcast. The series was based on my upcoming resource book to highlight the significance of my nonprofit, guide the audience through the book chapters, and show how to become involved in our initiatives. Each podcast provided valuable market research and increased community engagement. From the revenue generated and market research analysis, Head to Speech was able to create programs and products that met the needs of our audience. We experienced massive growth when we became a nationally recognized continuing education provider for our professional association, with over 223,000 members and affiliates.

Going into our third year, I lead the Board of Directors and staff members who have helped our volunteer community to grow through our Interprofessional Task Force Summit speakers and Ambassadors who helped us with Brain Workouts and Concussion Recovery Care Packages. All the hard work within the first three years led us to receive our first $5,000 grant to expand our programs and partner with other community organizations. We received more invitations for media appearances, speaking and publishing requests, and exhibitor experiences. We were able to establish a solid foundation for business sustainability and growth. By our 2nd interprofessional task force summit, we had five universities represented, nine speakers, three sponsors, and one athletic partner. We awarded six student scholarships and raised donations so four students could apply for a scholarship to attend the next summit.

I was ultimately accepted into leadership development programs at my university and through the American Speech-Language-Hearing Association due to my position at Head to Speech and my ability to clearly state my brand story and explain my cause, purpose, vision, and mission. I became a nationally recognized leader, public speaker, and author due to my social impact strategy and my abilities to execute my social impact strategy and health communications plan effectively.

WHAT YOU DON'T KNOW ABOUT ME

What I'm sure you don't know about me is that I founded BIA Communications simultaneously while working on my doctoral degree. I produced my first image management talk show for two years before I went into my period of solitary to write my dissertation. As I was becoming an entrepreneur, one of my brand strategies was not to wait to build my brand. I believed that I had to start, although I was not ready. I knew I shouldn't wait until everything was perfect. I learned from doing and trial and error, which was difficult because I had not fully grown into my purpose yet. As a result, my brand appeared misaligned with my professional life and inconsistent due to the stressors of my doctoral program.

People began to recognize the work I was doing with my show. Consequently, my mentor asked me, "How are you going to monetize your show?" I did not have a consistent production or profitable plan, nor was my brand aligned with social impact. I was producing the show, booking guests, and working with publicists, where everyone I interviewed back then has proven themselves as profitable influencers today. Some of the most notable guests came from professional associations and networks for coaching and speaking professionals in the image, communications, health, wellness, and affluent lifestyle industries. I realized how much work I was putting into it without little return. My show reached 100 subscribers and 3,792 views on YouTube. That was just the beginning without a real marketing strategy.

Once I restructured, rebranded, and realigned my purpose to my cause, vision, and mission, I achieved massive growth and sustainability. It is okay to do this. You should never feel embarrassed or ashamed that you have to make these three adjustments. We constantly evolve, and I thank God for growth! I am so happy that I did not allow my imposter syndrome to hold me back.

Restructure: Although I enjoyed what I was doing, I was approaching my talk show, authentic personal branding, and image consulting as a hobby rather than a business. I wasn't using any social marketing strategies at the time to connect my guests' causes with my audience to increase advertisement and sponsorships, nor was I monetizing my show beyond speaking engagements and branding photography. I found myself struggling to remain consistent with taping during my doctoral journey. Partially because when having a personal brand, everything requires you to run. So I put my show on hold and focused on Head to Speech using an organizational structure rather than being a sole proprietor.

I restructured BIA Communications as a social enterprise, which ultimately changed how I conducted business, fine-tuned my niche area, created my signature offerings, and charged for my worth and results rather than selling my time using hourly rates. The personal branding, coaching, and speaking industries are also very competitive and overly saturated, which makes a case for discovering your authenticity and using social impact branding to demonstrate to your ideal audience which causes matter the most to your brand and how it will specifically help them.

Rebrand: One of the problems was that my talk show wasn't aligned with social impact. I now realize the opportunities I missed to leverage my guests and raise awareness around the causes they cared about. After I graduated with my doctoral degree, I re-branded The Tabia Pope Show into BIA BRAND with Dr. Tabia Pope. BIA BRAND was now a trademarked brand linked to my purpose, cause, vision, and mission. Both BIA Communications and Head to Speech were created for different purposes but support each other for a common mission: to promote image, communications, health, wellness, and lifestyle causes and contemporary issues, as well as partner with business owners, social entrepreneurs, and influencers. The success I gained from my Head to Speech helped to simultaneously build BIA Communications' portfolio, organizational mindset, and business relationships. I felt empowered to link products, services, programs, and courses produced by BIA Communications to my social impact because of it!

Realign: I had to align what I do and all I have to offer as a brand to make it make sense to me, those within my community, and those with whom I wanted to help. I had to figure out how I was going to truly help them. My processes were all over the place at first. I had to streamline everything so my businesses aligned with my purpose, causes, vision, and mission. I didn't want to feel like I had two businesses. You can't be everything to everybody. Everyone isn't going to resonate with your causes or what you are trying to do for your community. I had to find a way to align what I had to offer with the right audience and the tools I needed to create to reach them more efficiently. I had to find a way to self-package my skills and businesses so I wasn't overwhelmed. Aligning my brands helped to find common ways that they could support one another in achieving the overarching goals and objectives I had set out for myself. I was successful because I committed to the process, even if it felt like I was taking a few steps backward.

Now, my businesses are packaged into signature programs and synched through an onboarding process. For example, if you want to work with me through my signature therapy, coaching, consulting, and speaking programs, you are directed to my LLC. My LLC provides services to Head to Speech when our leadership, Ambassadors, and volunteers need on-camera communication skills and image enhancement coaching or the organization requires social impact branding and video marketing strategies to raise awareness and donations through campaigns. On the other hand, Head to Speech only supports educational, scientific, and charitable initiatives. We conduct all continuing education and professional development training specifically towards our cause through the 501(c)(3).

BIA Communications now creates health communication campaigns and interviews for other social entrepreneurs and influencers in image, communications, health, wellness, and affluent lifestyle management. When I speak at masterminds or conduct workshops, I talk about authentic personal branding, social impact branding, and social responsibility but also reference my own businesses as examples and social proof of my massive growth and sustainability. I am empowering the audience to go out and create social enterprises and nonprofit organizations, get involved with charities, and brand themselves in a meaningful way.

WHY I AM SO COMMITTED TO HELPING YOU

Because of my experiences, I am committed to guiding you through the process that I took to align my brand with social impact. I was inspired through these challenges to develop a 5-step alignment method that helps you to understand my lessons learned, the processes I used, and the short-and-long term benefits of aligning your brand with social impact for massive growth and sustainability. I hope that by sharing my process, it will help you discover how to connect your purpose to your cause, vision, and mission. I am committed if you are committed to completing the following steps:

1. ALIGN Your Brand Values to your Cause, Purpose, Vision & Mission

2. ALIGN Your Brand with Social Impact Strategy

3. ALIGN Your Strategy to Your Market Research

4. ALIGN Your Research to Inform Your Massive Growth

5. ALIGN Your Growth with Packaging & Selling Your Brand Story

Chapter 1 will give you an overview of each step and the expected outcomes. As you read through the chapters, I promise you that you will begin to understand the steps necessary to grow throughout the process! As you align your brand with educational, scientific, and charitable initiatives, you will fully realize your purpose, cause, vision, and mission.

Educational initiatives: Align your brand with educational initiatives by producing public awareness campaigns, raising awareness, or providing access. You may want to establish a social mission with clear goals and then go on to create a public service announcement showcasing your values. You may go from hosting Ambassador training through workshops, retreats, or summits to exhibiting at national and international conferences and conventions. You may go from carrying out an advocacy agenda by meeting with and writing to local county council members about improving lives and strengthening your community impacted by your cause to participating in the political process to advance policies impacting your mission.

Scientific Initiatives: Align your brand with scientific initiatives by conducting focus groups to learn more about your community's opinions and needs. You may go from devising research questions to discovering the latest technology that supports your audience. You may go from creating a diverse career pathway for future researchers to scientific posters, presentations, and publications on your area of social impact. You may go from leading an interprofessional task force of diverse industry thought leaders, influencers, and builders to establishing an association, endowment, or foundation.

Charitable Initiatives: Align your brand with charitable initiatives by allocating funding or resources to innovators, nonprofits, small businesses, or startups dedicated to carrying out your mission. You may start by organizing fundraisers or care package drives to work your way up to developing a social responsibility program that allows your employees to match donations. You may go from working with your clients one-on-one to expanding your offerings to include support group counseling. You may go from hosting a community outreach event that expands its reach regionally, nationally, or even internationally.

ALIGN YOUR BRAND WITH SIGNATURE SOCIAL IMPACT OFFERINGS

Sell everything you know about your cause: My breakthrough came from transforming my dissertation research into an awareness campaign that later became a non-profit organization. I had to learn how to create my signature social impact offerings within these three areas. My experiences also showed me how powerful it is to align your brand with other brands supporting your educational, scientific, and charitable initiatives.

As I started to see my own results, I began to speak more and more about it. I was invited to speak to various audiences ranging from faculty and university students with image, communications, health, wellness, and lifestyle-related programs to business owners enrolled in professional development programs. For faculty and students, I focus on transforming their intellectual property from their personal and professional assignments into a brand with social impact. For business owners, I focus on venturing into social entrepreneurship and developing social responsibility initiatives to grow and scale their brands in this way. One of the highest return on investment (ROI) decisions they can make is engaging in social impact initiatives within their community, creating content that raises awareness, and donating their proceeds to the issues that matter the most to their brand, special interests, clientele, and underserved populations.

I ask them, What is your niche? What is your overall goal with your personal brand? What do you want to be known for from having a private practice? They usually tell me they want to be known as an advocate, educator, influencers, industry thought leaders, consultants, authors, communication and wellness expert, and so forth for their specializations. One of the takeaways from my experiences with private practice owners is when they make the connection between their private practice services and the causes associated with their services. I help them see the value in aligning their brand with social impact by reimagining what a private practice should look like. It is also a huge win when they begin to understand the benefits of other structures, such as nonprofit organizations and social enterprises. Any leader, business owner, or influencer should also transform their intellectual property into a brand with social impact. Your experience is valuable and will change lives as a social entrepreneur.

I really enjoy the call and response when I tell them to sell everything they know about their cause! So, I'm going to tell you the same thing. Say it with me, "Sell everything you know about your cause!" Start by taking ONE topic related to your cause and repurpose it into multiple campaigns, programs, products, services, and charity events that you can package, promote and sell to generate awareness and passive revenue.

Another group of social entrepreneurs I enjoy working with is our doctoral scholars with a passion for researching problems and their causes within their profession and community. I get asked all the time to mentor doctoral students who are either just starting to think about their topic, form their research questions, or explore the benefits of having a doctoral degree as they have made it through their journey. I enjoy introducing them to social entrepreneurship and providing them with a nontraditional career pathway that provides different alternatives to using their background and experiences. For example, I encourage them to use their knowledge of research methods as a social impact branding advantage.

I quickly started receiving client requests to work with me because I wrote a post in a community of higher education professionals about my own process to transform my dissertation, teaching, and research experience into a nonprofit organization. At the time, my story resonated with 160 other community members and received 46 comments. Comments ranged from those who recognized my work as great to those who thanked me for speaking to their souls and thanked me for just sharing the tips. Some commenters were already transforming their dissertation or capstone projects into nonprofit organizations; others reached out to learn how. This was when I knew I needed to write this book!

STRATEGIC PLANNING LEADS
TO RESULTS

Behind-the-Scenes of my Strategy Sessions: One of my clients was a Doctor of Philosophy (Ph.D.) student, a marriage and family counseling therapist, a practice owner, and a fitness gym owner who was very confident and clear on what her purpose, causes, vision, and mission were. She had already established her brand colors, brand photography, and website. She was very visible on social media. Consequently, she had two brands that needed to be merged into a synched brand. Her pinpoint of difficulty was that she needed to go back and trademark, copyright, create systems, streamline, and outsource all of her business's technical aspects because she was overwhelmed. She also struggled with securing the right type of visibility to showcase her social impact.

Although preparing for graduation, she was also finding the time to balance her businesses and family and preparing for massive growth using automated systems and online funnels for her programs. We strategized on how to restructure, rebrand and realign her new brand based on her dissertation and businesses with social impact. We also created programs and products to help her achieve multiple income streams with her educational, scientific, therapeutic, or charitable initiatives. She wanted to focus on raising awareness, having real in-depth conversations with her audience, and sharing experiences.

During our strategy session, my client stated, "I want to streamline my ideas. This is my goal!" I knew what she meant. She wanted to understand how to align her programs and products to her brand, which would give her more clarity with content creation. She wanted accountability and permission to do what she knew she needed. I got excited when I heard her come to the realization that she needed to start integrating, unifying, incorporating, or even organizing what she was doing within her business to what she was doing within her community. That showed me that she was ready for the alignment process. At the end of each strategy session, we would visualize and map out the next step in the process. When she realigned her brand, I knew she would be highly successful. She planned to launch a new arm of her business.

Committing to your audience: To assess where she was within the process, I started by asking her the following questions: Who are your audiences? What are your top 3 programs, products, and needs? Key groups are too broad, so we had to narrow them down and focus on a particular individual that needed her programs and products.

Social enterprise business model: There is a demand for aligning your brand with social impact. My client is driven by purpose. She shows how her programs and products impact her broader community and brings societal value. She is not alone. Approximately 3 in 4 millennials and Gen Zers are taking action to positively impact their communities (Deloitte, 2020). According to research conducted by Project Management Institute in 2020, 87% of leaders delivering meaningful change say that social impact is a concern for their brand.

I told my client that simply wanting to do good is not enough. She needs to utilize a social enterprise business model that aligns her brand with social impact around her cause, vision, and mission. While she believed she was outperforming other brands by simply aligning her brand with social impact, she also needed to incorporate social impact branding into her planning.

Social enterprises typically change industries, whereas non-profits choose to change a particular set of people (Mehta, R., 2019). My client wanted to sell products and services that advanced her social cause. We focused on structuring her business just like commercial businesses, with a business model, cost structure, and consumer base. I strategized with her to move beyond only focusing on donations because no revenue creation of any sort can be made. I cautioned her that when donations started decreasing, then her organization could not sustain itself.

Determine what to measure to understand your audience, the result your brand wants to achieve for massive growth, and the influences that impact the process and results. Your market research informs your ability to make not only a positive impact on your patients, clients, or customers but also on their families. I provided her with coaching on how to dive deeper into what she wanted to know about her audience and the results she wanted to achieve with the information. By doing so, she had to describe how her audience's perceptions depended on other independent variables, such as their demographics or experience with counseling and therapeutic interventions.

Learning the methods needed to measure the social impact of your educational, scientific, or charitable initiatives. According to the research, 69% of social impact brands rely on interviews or meetings with key groups within the community, whereas 68% use social listening and customer feedback. Furthermore, 65% use survey or questionnaire assessment compared to 59% who use health and socio-economic data. 80% of brands with methods for measuring social impact improve their social impact outcomes (Project Management Institute, 2020).

Facing Your Fears: I had my client ask herself, "Am I ready to face the positive and potential negative impacts of my brand? Her services may not be accessible to all populations who need her services within her community. This may have caused the underserved community to have negative perceptions of her brand. I told her not to feel discouraged but motivated that she realigned her brand with social impact.

I was also faced with addressing my client's barriers in order to fully align her brand with social impact. At the same time, I had to counsel her to overcome her fears and provide strategies to overcome the barriers unique to her situation. It is normal to have anxiety. It is normal to feel uncomfortable when doing something different. You know the only way to grow is to step outside your comfort zone.

We all feel like we lack something preventing us from achieving massive growth and sustainability. There will be highs and lows when you have to face these barriers head-on. Personally, going through these challenges helped to bring out my creativity. I encouraged my client to stay focused on completing what I have coined "BIA BRAND work." I empowered her to stay committed to the process. She started to see the results when she stayed committed to the process.

Leverage in-kind donations: Grants take time to manifest, so there were three questions that I wanted my client to think about and answer immediately. I asked her, "How was she going to utilize her existing community and their services, products, and programs to achieve massive growth?", "How was she going to create a community that provided in-kind donations?" and "How was she going to create memorable experiences that not only generated revenue but also showed how appreciative she was of her donors, fundraisers, and volunteers for their commitment and added value to her brand with social impact?

We then explored the in-kind donations, revenue-generating events, and unique experiences that she could create and invite community partners to host, donate, or deeply discount fees associated with the experience. We also explored how her social impact-driven brand could use different donation structures to give back to her cause or start donating to other organizations whose mission aligns with their brand values, purpose, cause, vision, and mission.

In order to maximize her donation potential, she needed to embrace creative and diverse fundraising alternatives to monetary contributions, such as products and services. She was able to offer her community the opportunity to participate in her organization's mission by donating in-kind donations regardless of their ability to donate financially. Pop-up shops and garage sales work well collecting and reselling donated items, such as clothing, arts and crafts, books, electronics, kitchen goods, toys, instruments, furniture, etc.

Another in-kind resource I recommended to my client was creating a task force, advisory board, or mastermind community consisting of professionals to receive pro-bono advice and high-quality services for her teaching academy, therapeutic interventions, and community outreach program. By doing this, she was also lowering or completely eliminating the costs associated with hiring employees or freelancers for work such as website or graphic design, fundraising, community engagement and growth, event planning, donor outreach, and Ambassador or volunteering coordination. I highly encouraged my client to conduct her own market research inside her community because it consists of highly successful professionals from her specific audience. This type of in-kind contribution should be considered a mutually beneficial partnership with clear expectations and time commitments.

Generate Revenue with Events: I explained to my client that curating experiences for her community could range from fundraising rewards, incentives, and VIP benefits to exclusive educational, celebratory, promotional, and networking events. She had to devise a partnership and sponsorship plan by deciding if she would use her community members or corporations as partners and sponsors. She had to decide which type of in-kind donations she would use for product pool, giveaways, raffles, door prizes, live or silent auctions, or year-round drives. She also had to ask her sponsors if they could provide event space, hospitality services, or supplies, such as tables, chairs, tents, food, and technology equipment.

Align your products with your cause and social responsibility initiatives: I explained to my client that she needed to start thinking about how she would use her products and the products of other brands to raise funds for her cause. She then had to match the donation structure that best aligned with her brand values, purpose, vision, and mission. We focused on developing a service-driven product strategy. She also had to explain how her products included diversity and inclusion, where the product materials came from, and whether the products and packaging were reusable or recyclable. We devised a storyboard to communicate the style and messaging of her brand values.

Donation structures for giving back to social enterprises: According to Givz, there are five ways to use products as a means to give back to your cause. The more products brands sell, the more product brands donate. As they grow, their giving and social impact within their community grows. One-on-one giving or one purchase equals one donation, where for each product purchased, the brand will donate either the same product or monetary value to your cause. A flat-rate donation is when a fixed amount is donated to your cause when the customer makes a qualifying purchase. A brand can also agree to donate either a percentage of sales or a percentage of profits to your cause. Lastly, a brand can determine designated products where they will create specific products or product lines to be donated, as well as designate how the funds will directly support your cause.

How long does it take to achieve massive growth and sustainability? The massive growth my client experienced in just one year takes the average social entrepreneur, business owner, or influencer two to three years or more to build. Many brands become truly successful after seven to ten years (Freshbooks, 2019). Consequently, the National Center on Charitable Statistics reveals that approximately 30% of nonprofits are not able to sustain themselves after ten years. Furthermore, Forbes found that more than half of brands without a strategic plan do not feel that "there are systems in place to ensure all stakeholders clearly share the vision and 'brand' of their nonprofit."

The work I did with my client helped to make sure

that this did not happen. My client's immediate impact included being able to successfully complete the registration forms for her incorporation. She was able to do this because we created a strategic plan and worked on aligning her purpose with her cause, vision, and mission into a cohesive statement.

The social impact stats provide indicators of successful outcomes for her programs and products. We projected an increase in sales revenue by up to 20% and an overall brand enhancement in reputation and visibility by 11%. Furthermore, we projected that every dollar she poured back into her community would generate six dollars in increased sales revenue (Fairchange, 2019 and IO Sustainability and Babson Innovation Lab, 2015).

My client's market research also paid off big time! She used her research to create packages that informed her stakeholders of her brand assets and social impact. By doing so, she decreased the risk of lacking alignment between what her partners, sponsors, and donors feel is important and what is actually being accomplished. Once partners, sponsors, consumers, and donors feel their contributions are being wasted, you run the risk of losing their revenue. According to Engage for Good (2022), 97% of companies consider brand and mission alignment as the top factor in partnership selection. Therefore, by consistently working towards her social impact visibility, she increased the number of corporate sponsorships.

With increased revenue, she was able to hire the production team that she needed to capture her programs. She went from producing zero public service announcements to securing several media appearances and speaking engagements within one year. She produced a PSA for her national convention exhibition and appeared in a segment discussing her upcoming community event. With the increased revenue, she was able to hire an events coordinator to ensure she was able to focus on community engagement. She increased the number of speakers and attendees. She increased the tickets of her retreat from hundreds to thousands of dollars.

All of the increased revenue eventually led to her hiring staff to handle operations and outsourcing tasks. There was an increase in her reach within her community. There was a progression in the capacity building to make the type of social impact she envisioned nationally and globally. According to the Business and Sustainable Development Commission (2017), over time, my client stands to gain a 5 to 15-year advantage over other brands who do not align their brand with social impact.

CHAPTER 3

ALIGN YOUR BRAND WITH SOCIAL IMPACT

Determine **where you are within the process**: I have given you an inside look into my process and how I work with clients to accelerate their massive growth and sustainability. Now, I want you to consider how this 5-step process applies to you.

Step 1: ALIGN Your Brand Values to your Cause, Purpose, Vision & Mission

Step 2: ALIGN Your Brand with Social Impact Strategy

Step 3: ALIGN Your Strategy to Your Market Research

Step 4: ALIGN Your Research to Inform Your Massive Growth

Step 5: ALIGN Your Growth with Packaging & Selling Your Brand Story

- If you are emerging within the process, then steps 1-2 are a good start.

- If you are expanding within the process, then steps 3-4 are a good start.

- If you already feel you are an influencer but still need help with visibility, then the 5th step is where you should start.

The first step in my 5-Step Process is to demonstrate how your brand values are aligned with your cause, purpose, vision, and mission and other brands with commonly shared brand values that can further your brand purpose, cause, vision, and mission. During this process, you will analyze the alignment between your brand values and cause in order to determine what part of your brand is a nonprofit, not-for-profit, or for-profit.

The second step is to complete a social impact strategy action plan that will also help your brand measure how well it is addressing the problem and its causes for a specific audience, raising awareness within key groups and communities, and amplifying its brand message through the use of various channels.

The third step is to measure the effectiveness of your brand's social impact strategy through market research. The evaluation process provides key insights and themes about your audience, as well as how well the channels used are meeting long-term performance outcomes and the ability to achieve massive growth and sustainability by staying ahead of the news and trends.

The fourth step is to assess your brand assets and align your research to inform your relationships with donors, partners, and sponsors, which leads to increasing your revenue and achieving massive growth and sustainability.

The fifth step is to dive deep into your brand identity and the approaches your brand can take to create content that accelerates your brand's storytelling and how it is aligned with social impact. During the process, your social impact strategy and market research will be leveraged by the packaging and selling of your brand story using various forms of media.

At the end of the five steps, I will provide you with an in-depth assessment that identifies which skills are needed for each stage, which strategies will help you achieve massive growth, and the level of sustainability each stage brings to your business, social enterprise, or nonprofit organization.

ALIGNMENT ACCELERATOR: Inside the **Align your Brand with Social Impact Accelerator**, we prepare you mentally for the 5-Step Process through visualization, manifestations, and affirmations. We explore how it feels to be in alignment and how it feels to be misaligned. We will discuss my favorite takeaways from my own experience in aligning my brand with social impact. One of the most important takeaways is to do this process now and do it afraid! We explore how this process requires vulnerability when sharing what to do and what not to do to accelerate your process. We also explore how to overcome the fears and challenges of aligning your brand with social impact, including getting others to see your vision and gaining the perspectives of others to expand your vision.

You will work through scenarios that help you build your community of board members, advisory board, task force, mastermind group, ambassadors, or volunteers. We will explore the power of board alignment and its critical roles in helping to expand your purpose, cause, vision, and mission. Many of the challenges address how to bring your community along during the emerging and expanding stages of your social enterprise or nonprofit organization. We celebrate each milestone along the process to honor where you are now and where you are going next.

Not only will you be ready to face the issues that may arise head-on, but you will also begin to develop skills and knowledge beyond direct clinical practice, including screening, assessment, or treatment. Through the use of thought questions, we explore your social impact strategy, including advocacy and outreach, education, collaboration, counseling, and prevention and wellness. You will learn how to leverage these skills to have a far greater reach and impact on those you work with and your community.

You will have access to case studies of educational, scientific, and charitable initiatives. You will also have access to examples of social responsibility initiatives specifically for business owners, social entrepreneurs, and influencers in the image, communication, health, wellness, and affluent lifestyle industries.

Once you go through these examples, you will be expected to generalize terms and messages to reach the masses, align your fundraising strategy with multiple revenue streams and discover your signature social impact area to develop, implement and evaluate offerings through programs, courses, products, or services.

One of the main points that will be stressed is to sell everything you know about your cause! We start by taking ONE topic related to your cause and repurposing it into multiple campaigns, programs, products, services, and charity events you can package, promote and sell to generate awareness and passive revenue. You will have access to examples of my own signature offerings and other offerings that allow you to spend more time on your actual social impact mission than having to focus entirely on donations and grants. We will also explore the importance of protecting your million-dollar ideas. As we dive deeper, we focus on which programs, courses, products, or services your audience needs. As you create the offerings, we explore the methods needed to measure the social impact of your educational, scientific, or charitable initiatives.

We use client case studies to explore the social enterprise business model, how to think like a nonprofit and act like a social enterprise, what it means to commit to understanding your audience, and the results and influences that impact the process.

CHAPTER 4

STEP 1: ALIGN Your Brand Values to your Cause, Purpose, Vision & Mission

From the beginning of this book, we have focused on the reason for beginning this journey towards aligning your brand with social impact. You have been able to focus on your purpose. You know who your brand is, what your brand does, why your brand matters, and why your brand is meaningful to other people. You have also been able to think about where you need to start to receive the type of support to move through my 5-step process.

The first step in my 5-step process is to align your brand values to your cause, purpose, vision, and mission. You will directly impact your cause by investing in the development of your brand values. You will be able to evaluate your impact based on your purpose, vision, and mission. This first step is all about diving deeper into finding the commonly shared brand values with individuals, businesses, organizations, or institutions that your brand needs to address your cause and remain loyal to your purpose, vision, and mission.

BRAND VALUES

Guiding light: Your brand values will guide the development, implementation, and evaluation of your awareness campaigns, services, programs, products, and selections of your board of directors, staff members, Ambassadors, volunteers, partners, and sponsors. There is so much power in each and every one of the one-word values that you use to build your reputation, mutually beneficial relationships, community outreach, and annual reports of our social impact. Never negotiate or compromise your brand values. They are the standards that you will hold everyone to. Your brand values will hold them accountable.

For example, you create a scholarship and diverse career pathways program to strengthen institutions that teach health and wellness professionals in order to reduce inequalities of health and wellness professionals from multicultural populations, ensure they receive a quality education, and further their economic growth. You craft messaging about the six key principles guiding how your nonprofit organization operates on your website and educational promotional materials. Those brand values are philanthropy, education, diversity, equity, economics, and empowerment.

CAUSE

Align Your Brand Values with a Cause: As you develop a deep understanding of the problem and its causes, you need to align your brand with causes that fit your values. You want to make your services, programs, and products more purposeful and meaningful to your audience. Having good reasoning for choosing your cause helps to make your cause feel more authentic to your brand. Your positive impact will feel like a natural extension of your brand because your audience understands your connection to your cause.

PURPOSE, VISION, MISSION

Purpose: Purpose keeps your brand focused on why it is inspired to make a difference, vision aligns your brand with your goals and objectives, and mission empowers how your brand will accomplish it. **Vision:** Vision defines your goals and sets the expectations of what you will experience when you align your vision and mission with your purpose. **Mission:** Your mission includes the decisions your brand makes to align your brand with social impact. Aligning your brand's mission with social impact requires you to hone in on your overall purpose for starting your organization. You will use your mission statement as a guide to constantly refer back to your mission.

Aligning your cause to your purpose, vision, and mission will help you determine how to structure your brand to achieve massive growth and sustainability. You have to have a strong purpose to attract directors, advisors, volunteers, or staff members. You need to have a powerful vision in order to lead them. You have to have a compelling mission statement in order to influence your messaging, partner, and sponsor selections, and donor and fundraising purchase decisions. Your goals or the specific aims you complete help to achieve your purpose. These goals are measured and tracked by objectives to help manage your progress. The foundation upon which you build needs to be solid.

Determining the Right Structure: Analyze the alignment between your brand values and cause by determining what part of your brand is a nonprofit, not-for-profit, or for-profit. Your brand values may not have a strong alignment with furthering a social cause to provide a public benefit. You need a strong alignment with a cause to become a social enterprise or nonprofit. If you structure your business as a nonprofit organization, you also need a wider-reaching audience and to center your cause around regional and national advancement initiatives. If you have ever envisioned your brand becoming known for educational, scientific, and charitable initiatives, then you qualify as a nonprofit. Most foundations, associations, colleges and universities, research institutions, and religious organizations are nonprofits. However, you don't have to structure your business this way to make a social impact. You must explore all of the ways that you can align your brand with social impact.

I believe you have to understand your brand's purpose and weigh the pros and cons. If you want to run a "grassroots" local organization or a social club that runs solely to meet the goals of your members, then consider a not-for-profit organization. If you rather generate profits to advance the organization and not for the owners, then structure your business as a nonprofit or not-for-profit. If you want to maximize revenues to receive compensation, then structure your business as a nonprofit or for-profit organization. Nonprofits must recycle the revenue back into the organization in the forms of salaries and honorariums, whereas for-profits distribute revenues above the profit line to owners and shareholders.

Consider your personality: Are you introverted or extroverted? If you are a private person, you may feel uncomfortable disclosing your organization's financial and operating information to the public. This is done so donors can understand what their contribution is being used for, such as programs or operational costs. Leading board members, advisors, and volunteers to accomplish your vision and mission requires a different skill set compared to donating proceeds from a service, product, or program. If your business requires certain types of start-up capital and business loans or wishes to operate without governance or tax implications, then a nonprofit or not-for-profit organization is not the right structure. Consequently, enjoying tax-exempt status from the Internal Revenue Service (IRS) is only reserved for nonprofits. Nonprofits are required to report their revenue, whereas not-for-profits are not.

How I utilize my 501(c)(3) versus my LLC: When I first started meeting with donors for Head to Speech start-up costs, I was asked a really profound question. "Why did you find Head to Speech as a nonprofit organization, not a for-profit company? I started off by stating what my cause was. I explained my vision and mission and how they were purpose and people driven. My purpose was to further my social cause to provide a public benefit to the sports community that was currently being underserved in my profession. My cause was to help students, professionals, and former athletes who were at risk of or had sustained concussions.

I adopted the nonprofit approach to reach more athletes and their support systems affected by cognitive-communication difficulties after sustaining a concussion. I then applied brain health and fitness principles to deliver key messages that key groups and community-at-large could relate to and participate in to increase interprofessional collaboration. I wanted all athletes to benefit from our programs regardless of their socioeconomic status because of the historical gaps in wealth, health disparities, literacy issues, cultural and linguistic differences, and cognitive assessment discrimination within multicultural populations. An individual or business that makes a donation is allowed to deduct their donation from their tax return. My organization, likewise, pays no taxes on any money received through fundraising.

What started off as a nonprofit is now also seen as a social enterprise. Our work extends way beyond being categorized as a charity. We are an educational institution running an online academy to educate speech-language pathologists, audiologists, and our allies on topics ranging from advocacy, performance, leadership, and innovation to brain injury, sports concussion management, cognitive-communication rehabilitation, and overall brain health. The revenue is distributed to further the advancement of the organization. Utilizing my background in research to collect data, write and publish annual reports has increased donor participation because they can see how their contributions are being used. Additionally, providing them with updated industry trends from the market research collected from our educational assessments.

I enjoy being a nonprofit leader because I have a passion for community outreach and being creative in how my organization holds fundraisers. I love the nonprofit culture because I rather focus on brainstorming ideas on how to help people and increase the social effectiveness of our organization's educational, scientific, and charitable initiatives rather than how to improve sales and productivity alone.

BIA Communications supports my nonprofit by specializing in digital media production, health communications, personal branding consulting for my talk show, digital products, coaching, speaking, and publications. I find more fulfillment in bridging my purpose for health and communications through BIA Communications. My LLC allows me to produce health communication tools using social marketing strategies. I also align my image management talk show with social impact by featuring social entrepreneurs, small business owners, and influencers who are aligning their own brands with social impact. The personal income I earn helps me to pursue business activities related to my nonprofit and to donate my time and profits right back into Head to Speech to run the organization. My LLC is separate and distinct from me as the owner. The personal income I receive is passed to me, and I report and pay taxes. I receive tax deductions for legitimate business expenses.

CHAPTER 5

STEP 2: ALIGN Your Brand with Social Impact Strategy

You have to identify what your problem is and its causes. Once you understand what is causing your problem, you now have to do something about it and focus on the problem itself. Shift away from what's causing it to what's wrong. You understand the problem and why it is extremely important for you to align your brand with social impact to solve the problem.

In this chapter, you will learn how to apply your problem and its causes to your brand and social impact strategy. Your social impact strategy is how your brand will achieve long-term performance outcomes, massive growth, and sustainability by remaining relevant and competitive.

You will establish a strategy to measure and amplify your brand's social impact. You will also develop, implement, and evaluate a health communication strategy to address the problem and its causes by increasing the knowledge and attitudes of your audience, key groups, and the community at large.

By the end of the chapter, you will identify the channels your brand wants to produce, as well as health communication tools from your perspective and your audiences, key groups, and the community at large. By doing so, you will then be able to transform your million-dollar ideas into a brand with social impact and improve lives within your community and around the world through social marketing strategies. Additionally, you will also be able to develop, implement and evaluate the effectiveness of the tools, initiatives, and resources used to achieve your goals and objectives.

Substantial and sustainable change requires a strong vision. A vision is defined and achieved through strategy; for brands pursuing social good, social impact strategy encompasses the goals, actions, and assessments used to enact and measure positive change. You need to understand how your brand brings about change, which factors contribute to making the change, and where your brand needs to partner with others to bring about change.

DEVELOP YOUR SOCIAL IMPACT STRATEGY

Let's use the Logic Model as your framework to identify the scope of your social impact program. For example, Your brand hosts an annual educational program. **Input:** Your inputs would include funding sources and the individuals helping to achieve the activities. **Direct control:** The metrics within your brand's direct control would be the amount donated, the number of hours the instructors and volunteers provided, and the percentage of individuals who attended the program. **Output:** The output of the educational program would be that the community was served through a seminar, which increased knowledge and changed attitudes and behaviors, and provided meals, which fed the community for attending.

The Short-Term Outcome: The short-term outcome would be to increase awareness, and the long-term goal would be to transfer knowledge, change attitudes towards their health, increase reporting and referral behaviors, and improve the quality of life for individuals in the served community. Your brand could also indicate progress based on established sources that have conducted market research based on this community and their knowledge, attitudes, and behaviors.

The Long-Term Outcome: The specific actions that were taken to host the annual educational program influenced the larger outcomes, such as the partnerships for the funding sources, the type of activities included in the program, and the background of the instructors and volunteers.

Themes: Immediately following the program, measure the social impact by collecting stories or having participants tell their stories using audio and visual formats. Describe the overall themes of the participants about the program. Their stories can help illustrate how inputs, activities, and outputs lead to the desired short-and-long term outcomes and ultimate social impact.

MEASURE YOUR SOCIAL IMPACT

How does your brand measure social impact? By measuring the impact of your social impact strategy, your brand will ensure its effectiveness and help your social impact grow. Knowing how effective your social marketing strategies and health communication tools are is crucial to securing various funding sources. Before measuring how well your brand is aligned with social impact, decide upon a framework to measure change within your organization, community, and customers. Make comparisons to similar organizations, sustainable development goals, and social return on investment. Understand how to measure the what, who, how much, contribution, and risk of your social impact strategy.

Once you carry out your strategy, consider the attribution or degree to which the specific actions brought about change. You will be able to put your work in the appropriate context when discussing the short-and-long-term goals. Don't be discouraged or conclude that your social impact strategy is ineffective if you do not see significant changes during the launching phase. It takes time to show the effectiveness of your social impact strategy.

Use every program as a learning tool to improve and grow. Stay the course and continue to use both qualitative and quantitative data. Hold your brand accountable for responding to the needs of the donors, volunteers, and participants through forums that provide your brand with opportunities to listen to feedback and provide resources for their needs, concerns, and ideas. By the end of the experience, your brand should create social impact reports demonstrating the process and the outcome data.

The Results of my own Needs Assessment Led to Increased Awareness and Revenue: I personally began developing a track record of success by using pre-and-post needs assessments for my educational programs. I utilized an educational needs assessment to assess individuals within my profession who were also in my special interest group. I wanted to know what topics were often not addressed enough or overlooked in academic and employment settings. My programs were designed to increase knowledge, change attitudes, and provide practical on-the-job training. In order to become a continuing education provider and launch our organization's online Academy, I had to demonstrate the effectiveness of the programs. My market research helped me identify initiatives that were not performing well and others I could change and improve upon. From my needs assessment, I also created an interprofessional task force mastermind group, summit, boot camp, journal club, Ambassador program, merchandise, and a subscription box.

DEVISE A HEALTH COMMUNICATIONS PLAN

Conveying your advocacy efforts, issues, challenges, and accomplishments to your audience through effective communication: According to Assist Creativelab, a health communications plan is the blueprint of your social impact strategy. It is also like a compass because it will point your social impact strategy in the right direction. It may change over time because you have to create new campaigns to expand your audience and access new types of communication and social marketing opportunities with partners and sponsors. After implementation, conduct ongoing assessments and revisions. It is better to deliver your message to the right audience to avoid wasting time and resources and ensure that your message is impactful and long-lasting. As we dive into aligning your brand with health communication tools, remember your Purpose, Audience, Message, channel, and relationships to **Distribute** your message.

Purpose: What does your brand need to communicate to your audience? Your brand's purpose may be to communicate about your advocacy agenda, programs to raise funds, recruitment opportunities for Ambassadors, or encourage consumers to purchase fundraising merchandise.

Audience: Your brand can not talk to all of the key groups involved at the same time. Different groups require different social marketing strategies and channels to deliver a message. Explore the demographics of the key groups through research and deliver messages based on their geographic location, age, gender, interests, habits, knowledge level, attitudes, and behaviors.

Message: Four key factors to compelling messaging are relatability, emotional tone, catchy hook, and desired impact using a call to action. Whoever is delivering the message has to be relatable to your audience. How they deliver a compelling message is also important. Your brand has to target the right emotion that will inspire your audience to act. Whether through body language or tone of voice, you need to understand the reactions to your messages. Your audience will want to receive the message if it is catchy, and they will remember the message in order to act.

Channel: How is your brand going to communicate your message? What does your audience read or listen to? Where do they frequently go to consume content? Choose the right channel to reach them and deliver your message for social change based on your audience's demographics. Health Communication tools include communication channels, such as awareness campaigns, print, and broadcast media, new social media channels and posts (i.e.,

Facebook Support Group, Twitter, and Instagram), live streaming, videos, reels, stories, tweets, podcasts, press releases, brochures, flyers, posters, handouts, news stories analysis, and documentaries. Educational content includes lectures, webinars, and seminars. Interactive tools include websites and emails. Interpersonal channels include (i.e. community led-meetings, biannual one-on-one meetings, and peer education). Professional channels and venues include (i.e., professional conferences and summits, online forums dedicated to interdisciplinary professions and issues, and organizational communication channels).

Distribute: Establish relationships to distribute your brand's message for social change. Find ways to link your message with other partners who cater to your audience. Connecting with influencers who support your message will increase your exposure and amplify the overall message for social change.

Health Communication Objectives for New Tools and Campaigns: Health Communication objectives are the intermediate steps towards achieving social impact outcomes. The health communication objectives are related to the critical group's knowledge, attitudes, and behaviors. The established relationship and partnership between the key groups will increase the likelihood of achieving health communication objectives. Communication objectives are needed to ensure that the communication needs of stakeholders and key groups are sustained over time. The existing levels of knowledge, attitudes, and behaviors will provide insight into which three objectives will take priority. However, all the communication objectives will be implemented in the health communication plan that addresses the mass media, new media, online events, interpersonal channels, professional channels and venues, and any other specific activity that targets the mass audience.

Identify the number one human and economic resource: Government agencies and associations are primarily responsible for establishing health communication objectives and strategies. They will be able to support your brand in developing health communication strategies.

Interprofessional education and collaboration: Interprofessional practice (IPP) is a framework that makes this collaboration more successful, whereas interprofessional education (IPE) helps students develop the skills needed to work on these interprofessional teams. Understanding the differences between Interprofessional education (IPE) and Interprofessional practices (IPP) is essential in how your brand works to achieve common goals as a means for solving various problems and complex issues.

You can achieve more together than you can individually. What I genuinely find noteworthy is that creating your own social enterprise or nonprofit organization ensures that you align your brand with the professionals within your network with whom you choose to work with and those within your community with whom you want to support.

Contemporary Trends, Issues, and Policies: Integrating policy and advocacy agendas of the government, associations, and national partners into your own social impact strategy will result in the alignment of actively monitoring what is happening and connecting the dots so your brand can see trends, share information, craft solutions, and mobilize for action. Your brand plays a vital role in influencing policies that support, strengthen, and protect the community that you serve.

Lack of adequate health communication tools: You may find that there is either a lack of adequate health communication tools for your audience. The tools may not mention or briefly mention a topic or professional. The tools may not include detailed descriptions or explanations. The tools may not reflect your cause, brand values, purpose, vision, or mission.

Establish a strong rationale for new tools: You will have to devote more time and resources to developing, implementing, and evaluating health communication tools. I want to emphasize that you can also modify existing health communication tools. You do not have to reinvent the wheel.

Bridge the gap between your brand and other entities: Agencies, associations, organizations, universities, corporations, social enterprises, and the community at large can all benefit from health communication tools.

Call to Action: Convey your advocacy efforts, issues, challenges, and accomplishments to your audience through effective communication. Determine what your brand is calling your audience to do. Is your audience being called to contact you, make a donation, join the community, learn more, become an Ambassador, increase the number of referrals, identify areas of concern, become a partner, change behaviors, increase knowledge, develop skills, become a trainer, or become a board member?

STEP 3: ALIGN Your Strategy to Your Market Research

In the previous chapter, you learned the keys to social impact strategy to address your audience's problem and its causes. You learned how valuable interprofessional education and collaborative practices are to understand the current contemporary issues, policies, and trends. You are beginning to think about implementing a health communication plan to use as your brand's compass to point your social impact strategy in the right direction. By strengthening your understanding of the process, you will implement tools that communicate your purpose to your audience and key groups and deliver and distribute your message through various channels.

You are now diving deeper into understanding the knowledge, attitudes, and behaviors of your audience and key groups as you progress through evaluating your social marketing strategies. Never underestimate the power of engaging and mobilizing your audience through market research. Market research will help your brand consider the social impact your brand is trying to deliver and how your brand will measure it. Your brand will determine the effectiveness of the health communication tools and campaigns, as well as evaluate the projected massive growth and any threats to sustainability.

Evaluate the Effectiveness of Active Health Communication Tools and Campaigns: Researching what already exists within your niche area allows you to develop or modify programming based on successful trends or toolkits. The following are questions to ask when investigating the effectiveness and examples of statements demonstrating the effectiveness of the health communication tools and campaigns.

Investigating the Effectiveness: As you hone in on a particular active health communication campaign, you have to investigate where you need to fill in the gaps. You may find that some professionals are left out of active tools and campaigns, which is problematic because your audience needs to know all the key groups and stakeholders involved in maximizing social impact, increasing knowledge, and changing attitudes. Campaigns evolve over time by moving from just addressing their audience's needs, roles, and responsibilities to providing education and increasing their awareness.

Evaluation Process: Your brand needs to understand how the new health communication messages, tools, and initiatives are integrated into the lives of key groups online and offline. Your brand has to react quickly to emerging or developing trends because it demonstrates not only how invested your brand is to the cause but also to the audience's needs and preferences. They will go to your brand to stay informed about everything related to your problem and its causes, evidence-based practice, recent media headlines, programs, products, or services. Your brand needs to find where there are breakdowns in messages, tools, and initiatives to ensure increased participation. Meeting on a quarterly meeting cycle will continue to foster a positive environment in which all key groups involved share, understand, absorb, and discuss the agenda set forth.

Conduct Market Research: Your brand will prepare to conduct market research using either focus groups, semi-structured interviews, or online questionnaires. **Focus groups:** Establish rapport with the group, and provide written agendas with built-in feedback reports to give each participant ample amount of time to share their thoughts. For example, PowerPoint presentations with built-in polling software and visual aids encourage participation and further learning directly or indirectly. **Semi-structured interviews** help maintain responsive communication and keep the team responsible for addressing the problems and issues. **Questionnaires:** Using a 5-point Likert scale can help to collect and analyze qualitative and qualitative data. The team should determine the questions, intended selected responses, and open-ended responses.

Intended or Unintended Outcomes: Health communication tools present intended and unintended outcomes due to contradictory beliefs, attitudes, and behaviors, as well as influences on being able to focus on the tools. It does make a difference in how long your audience has been exposed to the same messages. Your audience can become apathetic rather than empowered to increase their knowledge or change their attitudes and behaviors. Consequently, the ongoing messages may result in unnecessarily high concern on the part of your audience and those involved in the problem and its causes.

Monitoring Plan for News and Trends: Your brand needs a process for monitoring news and trends. There are three steps that need to be taken. The first step is tracking news and trends. The second step is publicly providing a monthly report, presentation, or distribution. The third step is creating a program or event that drives the conversation on the report that your brand produced, as well as showcases your process and progress in monitoring news and trends.

CHAPTER 7

STEP 4: ALIGN Your Research to Inform Your Massive Growth

In the previous chapter, we found that good social impact evidence can also help your brand make improvements, compare achievements with similar brands and communicate the difference your brand is making to be able to attract further donors, partners, and sponsors.

In this chapter, you will assess your brand assets and align your research to inform your relationships that lead to increasing your revenue. You will learn how to develop, implement and evaluate market research to use social marketing strategies in a way that intelligently informs how to increase your audience's knowledge and change their attitudes towards your important purpose, mission, and causes. Packaging your research and assets makes you more marketable to corporations, organizations, and educational institutions.

Align your research to inform your partnerships: The traditional way versus the way that highlights your assets. Usually, people develop a pitch and create an outdated sponsorship package with levels associated with prices.

Know the difference between Corporate Social Responsibility and Corporate Sponsorships and how they intersect: Corporate Social Responsibility should be treated as an established program or grant that you are vying to be a part of compared to Corporate Sponsorships that focus on whether or not your event aligns with their goals and existing program. According to Brand Yourself Better, Sponsorship involves a business relationship between two parties, where one party (sponsor) provides support through funding, resources, or services to the other party (beneficiary). The beneficiary, in return, allows access to the sponsor for rights and associations for commercial advantage.

Build an inventory of everything you are willing to sell: List some ways you can help your sponsors achieve their goals but don't list them as packages they have to buy. Show your sponsors how you've helped other sponsors achieve their goals by working with you. Get your leadership team, program team, marketing department, volunteers, and current sponsors together and ask them what they think you should be selling.

Not understanding your audience: Build a rapport with your audience by sending them a needs assessment or facilitating a focus group.

Making an ask without a relationship: Building an authentic relationship is critical to successful agreements. Ensure you are in touch with sponsors throughout the year, not just when you have a need.

Sponsor research: Ensure you find meaningful and innovative ways to engage sponsors. Create a customized sponsorship based on their needs.

Not having a clear understanding of how to access corporate social responsibility funding: Corporate social responsibility grants are highly competitive. They operate much like Foundation grants. Read Corporate social responsibility initiatives carefully and make sure they align with your goals and objectives. You must be able to connect your program to the company's corporate social responsibility initiatives.

Focusing heavily on just one fundraising source: Financial plan should include innovative ways to sustain donations. For example, a monthly or seasonal offering

Making assumptions: Making assumptions that "companies have lots of money to give away much money each year." Companies will not invest money into your charity because you are a charity. Companies invest money into charities that support their values. Demand a return on their investment. Focus on offering a big enough impact! Deliver what you promise!

Mutually Beneficial Partnerships: Give your partners the opportunity to voice for themselves what elements benefit them. Connecting with your community by sponsoring a one-off event should align with their own purpose, causes, vision, mission, and values. All of your events may have different audiences, be based on different themes, uplift your community in the most needed ways, provide unique opportunities to interact with your community and support different educational opportunities.

Your annual report: Let your sponsors know the total amount given in grants. They want to know the total number of programs and participants you had the previous year. Let them know the number of individuals, organizations, or businesses you supported through your programs.

Representing their interest: Knowing what your partner or sponsor is interested in will accelerate the process of achieving massive growth and sustainability. If a potential partner or sponsor lands on your website, provide them with several options they may be interested in. These options should range from brand awareness and educating their staff to connect with your community, recruiting your community, or generating social impact within your community.

Event Offerings: Potential alignment with another brand that wants your brand to educate their community will want to know about your one-off events, unique workshops, and self-study course offerings.

Opportunity "Opps" Page: Potential alignment with another brand that wants you to bridge the gap between access and opportunity will want to share an opportunity with your community.

Signature Packages: Intensive Days create a social impact immersion day (or two) where both brands experience each other's worlds.

The 6-12 month phased partner approach: Develop a program that aligns with both of your social impact goals and increases understanding and exposure of the aligned brand while building the skills and experience of your Ambassadors interested in their related industry.

CHAPTER 8

STEP 5: ALIGN Your Growth with Packaging & Selling Your Brand Story

In the previous chapter, you were given examples of social impact offerings to attract donors, partners, and sponsors that will increase your revenue and achieve massive growth and sustainability.

In this chapter, you will answer the following question, **What is my brand story?** The time is now to accelerate your brand's storytelling and how it is aligned with social impact to achieve massive growth and sustainability. Write down and visualize how you want to tell your brand story as you go through the brainstorming process.

This chapter requires you to reflect on your purpose, cause, vision, and mission in the present, past, and future. As you reflect, you are provided with an opportunity to devise a strategic plan that can be easily executed now because you understand your purpose, cause, vision, mission, audience, and tools needed to reach them. However, within this chapter, I also want you to think about how your brand benefits not just your audience but all of us.

You will use your social impact strategy and market research that you produced to align your growth with packaging your brand story using various forms of media. You will learn how to record your brand story using video and audio formats. Dive deep into your brand identity and the approaches your brand can take to create content.

One way I utilize my health communication experience for my image management talk show program is by coaching emerging and expanding social entrepreneurs on how to create video marketing campaigns. I integrated this concept into my nonprofit organization, where I work with student and professional organizations to produce Public Service Announcement Challenges. I have also featured students and professionals at my national convention exhibition booth as an interactive opportunity. Our Head to Speech Ambassadors produces PSAs to raise awareness of our cause by utilizing our motto, appealing to our allies, and advising our audience and their support systems.

The PSA Strategy: One of the benefits of being a nonprofit is that the organization can leverage for-profit advertising tactics for free through radio, television, online, and other media platforms! Creating a Public Service Announcement (PSA) does not have to be hard. However, it does have to talk to everyone rather than a specific target audience.

12 Videos To Package and Sell Your Brand Story: There are 12 videos that your brand should create to package and sell your brand story. They are the Public Service Announcement, Podcast or Radio Spot, Social Media Reel, Explainer Video, Product Demonstration Video, Social Responsibility Culture Video, Behind-the-Scenes Video, Customer Testimonial Video, Ambassador Profile Video, Web Series, Branded Mini-Documentary, and Short Film.

Storytelling through the use of an Anthology: There are also other forms of media that can be used for packaging and selling your brand, such as Anthologies. They provide a collection of smaller works, including short stories, essays, or poems. Additionally, they may also be a blend of different authors following a central theme or genre or a book of short stories compiled by the same author.

Focus on the why: I am here to help you understand your brand story and how your brand story will resonate with everyone connected to your cause, purpose, mission, and vision. Focus on why creating your brand story from a social marketing perspective is essential. You have to master your brand story to control the direction it takes your brand in aligning with social impact.

Creating a Passion Pitch: It's important for social enterprises to take time to craft their brand stories in a way that appeals to donors, partners, sponsors, and consumers. More than an "elevator pitch," social enterprises and non-profits need a "passion pitch" that incorporates clear intention, measurement standards, and transparency each step of the way.

ACCELERATE YOUR GROWTH

Go to **biabrand.tv** to take the *Align Your Brand with Social Impact Assessment* to discover where you need to start. Get on the waitlist for the next *Align Your Brand with Social Impact Accelerator* program. Let's apply everything you have learned by reading this book and apply it to my 5-Step Process to accelerate your massive growth and sustainability. During the accelerator program, you will complete modules designed for those who are emerging, expanding, and developing as influencers within the process. After taking this course, you will be able to do the following:

- Discover your purpose, cause, vision, and mission and leverage them into a social enterprise, non-profit, or corporate social responsibility entity and other opportunities in advocacy and outreach, education, collaboration, counseling, and prevention and wellness.

- Strategize to grow and scale your social enterprise or nonprofit organization through producing products, services, programs, or courses or increasing the number of partners, sponsors, and donors interested in addressing your educational, scientific, and charitable initiatives.

- Fast track the development, implementation, and evaluation of social enterprise, nonprofit, or corporate social responsibility initiatives that address environmental, philanthropic, diversity, equity and inclusion, and economic issues within the image, communications, health, wellness, and lifestyle industries.

- Take action by applying social impact branding strategies to a health communications and video marketing plan that can be used for community building and recruitment, raising awareness and donations, and maximizing exposure to your brand values, purpose, cause, vision, and mission through media appearances and speaking engagements.

- Work with BIA Communications to ensure you and your ambassadors are cameras ready for social impact branding photography, leadership development training, executive presence for meetings and networking opportunities on-and-offline, community-based programs and fundraising events, speaking engagements, and media appearances. Our services include on-camera communication skills and image enhancement coaching, media and influencer training by becoming a talk show guest on BIA Brand with Dr. Tabia Pope or becoming a part of our image management production and publication campaigns, including the following:

- Impact and Brand Management Talk Show Interviews, Branded Mini-Documentaries, and Anthology Campaigns related to image, communications, health, wellness, and lifestyle issues and social responsibility initiatives

- Awareness Campaigns and Public Service Announcement Challenges using Radio Spots, Podcasts, and Social Media Reels focused on local, national, and global community calls to action

- Social Impact Marketing Videos that showcase your brand and its community using signature offerings, including Explainer Videos, Product Demonstration Videos, Social Responsibility Culture Videos, Behind-the-Scenes Videos, Customer Testimonial Videos, and Ambassador Portrait Videos

ABOUT THE AUTHOR

Dr. Tabia Pope is a three-time Alumna of Howard University, where she earned her Doctor of Philosophy (Ph.D.) degree in Communication Sciences and Disorders. Her specialization is in medical speech-language pathology and neurogenic disorders, with clinical and research interests in brain injury, sports concussion management, and neuropsychology. She has many experiences ranging from health communications and social marketing to contemporary issues, policies, interprofessional education, and collaborative practices. Over the past decade, Dr. Pope has gone from being a struggling talk show host, speech therapist and doctoral student to becoming a Professor, social entrepreneur, and influencer. During this time, she founded BIA Communications as a Limited Liability Company (LLC) and Head to Speech, Incorporated as a 501(c)(3) nonprofit organization. She teaches others how to transform their million-dollar ideas into social enterprises and nonprofit organizations through her 5-Step Process. Dr. Pope currently raises awareness and donations for brain health, sports concussions and their effects on cognitive-communication skills. Additionally, serving as a Head to Speech Ambassador, on-camera communication skills and image enhancement coach, and BIA BRAND talk show host who raises awareness and donations for social impact issues related to image, communications, health, wellness, and lifestyle. She now has two businesses representing her brand within the community, but it wasn't always that way.

Websites: www.biabrand.tv

www.headtospeech.org

Subscribe on LinkedIn: BIA BRAND with Dr. Tabia Pope
linkedin.com/in/drtabiapope
linkedin.com/company/head-to-speech

YouTube: www.youtube.com/@biabrandTV

Instagram: @biabrandTV | @headtospeech

Facebook: BIA BRAND with Dr. Tabia Pope
Head to Speech, Incorporated

REFERENCES

Altman, I. (2016). Half of nonprofits are set up to fail --
How about your favorite? Retrieved from:
https://www.forbes.com/sites/ianaltman/2016/03/20/ha
lf-of-nonprofits-are-setup-to-fail-how-about-your-favor-
ite/?sh=109cf98b4619

Assist Creativelab. (2020, January 24). How to develop a
communication plan for social impact. Retrieved from:
https://creativelab.assistasia.org/social-impact-communi-
cation-plan/

Better Yourself Better. (December 30, 2020). How Does
Sponsorship Work? Retrieved from: https://brandyour-
selfbetter.com/blog/post/208450/how-does-sponsorship-
work

Business and Sustainable Development Commission
(2017). Better business, better world. Retrieved from:
https://d306pr3pise04h.cloud-
front.net/docs/news_events%2F9.3%2Fbetter-business-
better-world.pdf

Deloitte. (2020). Global Millennial Survey, Deloitte. Retrieved from: https://www2.deloitte.com/content/dam/Deloitte/global/Documents/About-Deloitte/deloitte-2020-millennial-survey.pdf

Engage for Good. (2022). Social impact statistics you should know. Retrieved from: https://engageforgood.com/guides/statistics-every-cause-marketer-should-know/

Fairchange. (October 31, 2019). 8 Benefits of maximizing your business' social impact. Retrieved from: https://www.fairchangeimpact.com/8-benefits-of-maximizing-your-business-social-impact/

Freshbooks. (2019). How long it takes for a small business to be successful: A year-by-year breakdown. Retrieved from: https://www.freshbooks.com/hub/startup/how-long-does-it-take-business-to-be-successful

Givz and Mayfield, D. (n.d.). How to align your brand values with a cause. Retrieved from: https://www.givz.com/blog/brand-values-with-a-cause

Mehta, R. (November 12, 2019). Should nonprofit organizations be considered as social enterprises? Retrieved from: https://www.linkedin.com/pulse/should-nonprofit-organizations-considered-social-rhea-mehta

Project Management Institute (2020). Why Social Impact Matters: Delivering Meaningful Change Through Projects. Pulse of the Profession.

Rochlin, S., Bliss, R., Jordan, S., and Kiser, C. (2015). Project RIO study: Defining the competitive and financial advantages of corporate responsibility and sustainability. Retrieved from: https://www.issuelab.org/resources/22448/22448.pdf

S, Tracy. (September 7, 2019). Nonprofits fail – Here are seven reasons why. Retrieved from: https://nanoe.org/nonprofits-fail/

Shopify. (2022, December 10). Nonprofit vs. not-for-profit: What's the difference? Retrieved from: https://www.shopify.com/blog/non-profit-vs-for-profit